One World

In the Country

Valerie Guin

Smart Apple Media

Note
about the series

One World is designed to encourage young readers to learn more about people and places in the wider world. The photographs have been carefully selected to stimulate discussion and comparison.

First published in 2004 by Franklin Watts
96 Leonard Street, London EC2A 4XD

Franklin Watts Australia
45-51 Huntley Street, Alexandria, NSW 2015

This edition published under license from Franklin Watts. All rights reserved.

Copyright © 2004 Franklin Watts.

Editor: Caryn Jenner, Designer: Louise Best, Art director: Jonathan Hair, Map: Ian Thompson
Reading consultant: Hilary Minns, Institute of Education, Warwick University

Acknowledgements: Tim Beddow/Hutchison: 18. Tony Binns/Easi-Images: 13. David Cummings/Eye Ubiquitous: 24t. Mark Edwards/Still Pictures: 26. Sarah Errington/Hutchison: 3, 16. Robert Francis/Hutchison: 24b. Gallo Images/Eye Ubiquitous: 10. Patricio Goycoolea/Hutchison: 12. Carlos Guarita/Still Pictures: 19. Jean Hall/Holt Studios: 20. Roger De La Harpe/Gallo Images/Corbis: 9. Juliet Highet/Hutchison: 15t. Jeremy Horner/Hutchison: 14. Wayne Hutchinson/Holt Studios: 11. L. Johnstone/Eye Ubiquitous: endpapers, 15b. P. Karunakaran/Holt Studios: 23. Roy Maconachie/Easi-Images: 21. J.C. Moschetti/Still Pictures: cover, 17b. Ray Pfortner/Still Pictures: 25. Bryan Pickering/Eye Ubiquitous: 6. Bill Ross/Corbis: 8. Sarah Rowland/Holt Studios: 22. Tony Souter/Hutchison: 7.

Published in the United States by Smart Apple Media
2140 Howard Drive West, North Mankato, Minnesota 56003

U.S. publication copyright © 2006 Smart Apple Media
International copyright reserved in all countries. No part of this book may be reproduced in any form without written permission from the publisher.
Printed in the United States of America

Library of Congress Cataloging-in-Publication Data

Guin, Valerie.
In the country / by Valerie Guin.
p. cm. — (One world)
ISBN 1-58340-695-6
1. Farm life—Juvenile literature. 2. Country life—Juvenile literature. 3. Natural history—Juvenile literature. I. Title. II. Series: One world (North Mankato, Minn.)

S519.G85 2005
630—dc22   2004052504

9 8 7 6 5 4 3 2 1

Contents

Our countryside

All around the world, there
is countryside. Countryside
is land that is away from
towns and cities.

This is a **map** of all the **countries** in the world. Read this book to find out about countrysides all over the world.

▶ This boy is walking in the countryside. In this book, you will see lots of different things in different kinds of countrysides.

Natural places

In the countryside, there are **natural** things such as trees and other plants. Many trees grow in this **forest** in Canada. It is autumn, and the leaves on the trees are turning from green to gold and orange.

Brightly colored wildflowers grow in this field in South Africa. These flowers are not planted by people. The seeds are scattered by animals and by the wind.

Wild animals

Different kinds of wild animals live in the countryside. This elephant family is feeding on the grass of the African **savannah** in Tanzania.

Rabbits live wild in many parts of the world. In Sweden, there are many fields and forests where rabbits can hop around.

Farm animals

Some animals in the
countryside live on farms.
This farmer in Spain keeps
sheep for wool and meat.

In many places, such as China, farmers use water buffalo to help on farms. At the end of the day's work, the water buffalo cool off in the river.

Growing food

Many different kinds of **crops** are grown on farms. These farm workers in Vietnam are planting rice in a field called a paddy. Rice is the most common food in the world.

Crops need time to grow and become **ripe**, then they can be **harvested**. These workers in France are picking ripe grapes.

This machine cuts ripe wheat in a field in the Ukraine. Wheat is used to make bread and other foods.

After the harvest

▲

Grassy plants that are used for food, such as wheat and rice, are called grain. These women in Sudan are separating out the part of the ripe grain that can be eaten. This is called winnowing.

These men in Chile are
putting ripe wheat into
a machine that
separates the grain.

Village life

▲

A village is a small town in the countryside. On market day, people gather to buy and sell fruit and vegetables that they have grown. This is a village market in Belgium.

In some villages, people prepare their meals together. These women in Nigeria are peeling a vegetable called manioc. They are preparing enough food for several families.

Country crafts

People often use **materials** from the countryside to make things for the home. This woman in Ireland uses willow from nearby trees to weave baskets.

This woman in Bolivia weaves wool into colorful cloth. The wool comes from a large farm animal called an alpaca.

▼

Special events

At a country fair, there are shows and competitions for people living in the countryside. These horses are pulling a cart around the show ring at a country fair in Britain.

Many people watch the
ox races that take place in
country villages in southern
India every summer.

Enjoying the countryside

These people are on a hiking trip in Peru, where there are well-marked mountain trails.

Campers have set up this tent on the side of a lake in Australia. The tent shelters the campers when they sleep outdoors.

This family in New Zealand has come to the countryside for a picnic. The boys are looking for fish and insects in the shallow river. They are being very careful, because they do not want to spoil the countryside.

Saving the countryside

The countryside must be protected
to keep it natural. These children
are picking up garbage from a
beach in the United States.

These children in Sri Lanka are on their way to plant new trees. The new trees will replace trees that have been chopped down.

All around the world

All around the world, there is countryside.

Canada

United States

Ireland
Britain
Spain

Peru

Bolivia

Chile

The countries that you have read about are shown in pink on this map of the world. Find the country that matches each picture in the book.

Belgium

Ukraine

Sweden

France

China

India

Sri Lanka

Sudan

Nigeria

Tanzania

South
Africa

Vietnam

Australia

New
Zealand

Glossary

countries   places with their own governments

crops   plants grown for food

forest   an area of land where many trees grow

harvest   to pick ripe crops

map   a drawing that shows where places are

materials   things used to make other things

natural   not made by people, but part of nature

ripe   ready to be picked or eaten

savannah   a grassy area of land in a hot place

Index